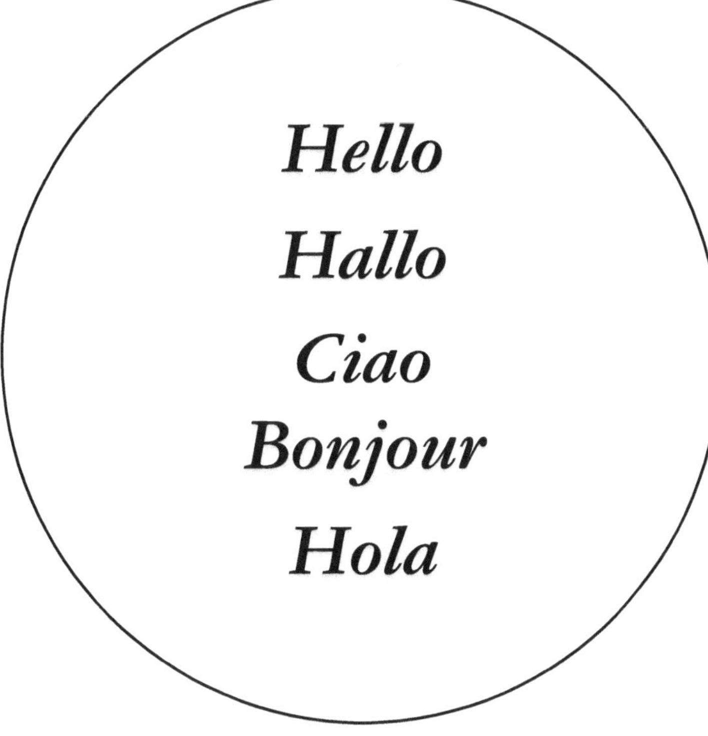

My Language Notebook belongs to

....

Language Level................

LISTENING

(German) *Guten Morgen*
(English) *Good Morning*

READING

(Italian) A Presto
(English) See you soon

SPEAKING

(French) S'il vous plait
(English) Please

WRITING

(Chinese) 晚安
(English) Goodnight

GRAMMAR

(Spanish) Gracias
(English) Thank you

VOCABULARY

(Portuguese) Tchau
(English) Bye

www.ingramcontent.com/pod-product-compliance
Lightning Source LLC
LaVergne TN
LVHW060258200726
843507LV00009B/1141